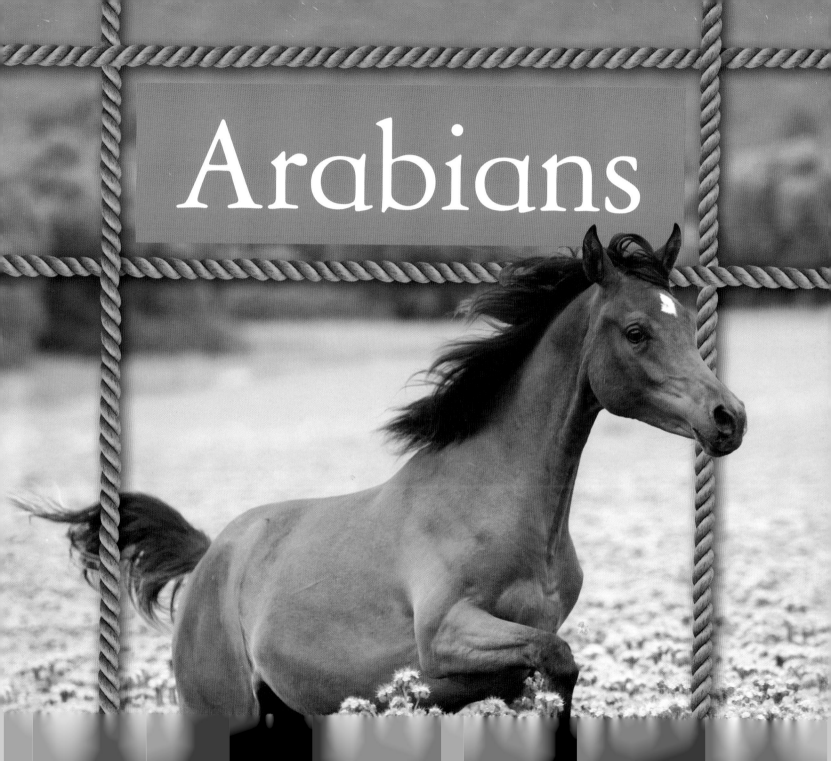

Arabians

The Child's World

Published by The Child's World®
1980 Lookout Drive • Mankato, MN 56003-1705
800-599-READ • www.childsworld.com

Acknowledgments
The Child's World®: Mary Berendes, Publishing Director
The Design Lab: Design
Jody Jensen Shaffer: Editing
Red Line Editorial: Photo Research

Photo credits
Alina Vincent Photography, LLC/iStock.com: 16; anakondasp/
Shutterstock.com: 15; Dozornaya /iStock.com: 20; Eric Isselee/
Shutterstock.com: 22-23; Joe Belanger/Shutterstock.com: rope;
Kerrick/iStock.com: 11; Makarova Viktoria/Shutterstock.com:
6; Olga_i/Shutterstock.com: 12; pirita/Shutterstock.com: 19;
robangel69/iStock.com: 9; Vaclav Volrab/Shutterstock.com:
horseshoes; Zuzule/Shutterstock.com: cover, 1, 5

ISBN 9781626870031
LCCN 2013947282

Printed in the United States of America
Mankato, MN
September, 2014
PA02249

ABOUT THE AUTHOR

Pamela Dell is the author of more than fifty books for young people. She likes writing about four-legged animals as well as insects, birds, famous people, and interesting times in history. She has published both fiction and nonfiction books and has also created several interactive computer games for kids. Pamela divides her time between Los Angeles, where the weather is mostly warm and sunny all year, and Chicago, where she loves how wildly the seasons change every few months.

CONTENTS

Fast, Strong, and Beautiful

The desert air is clear and hot. Nothing is moving. Suddenly, some horses come into view. They are light and fast, racing across the sands. Their flying hooves kick up a cloud of dust. There is no question what kind of horses these are. They are Arabians!

People in the Middle East had deep beliefs about Arabian horses. They had many stories about them, too.

Once, these beautiful horses were known only in the Middle East. Then other people learned of their speed, strength, and bravery. Today, Arabians are treasured throughout the world.

This Arabian is running in a field of flowers.

What Do Arabians Look Like?

No horse is more beautiful than an Arabian! Artists have always tried to capture this animal's look. Lots of paintings and photos show Arabian horses. They show the horses' fine heads and well-built bodies. The horses' necks form a graceful curve. Their coats shine like glass. Their eyes flash. Their thin, strong legs seem to dance when they move. Arabians have always had a proud, spirited look.

Many famous people have owned Arabian horses. The first U.S. President, George Washington, had Arabians.

In real life, Arabian horses look like nothing else. Their heads are shaped a little like a triangle. The heads are wide at the jaw. They narrow down to a small nose and mouth. Their foreheads seem to curve outward. Their ears are small and point forward. Their bodies are slim. Their feet are small, with hard hooves.

Male Arabians have smaller, pointier ears than the females.

This graceful Arabian is running on a fall day.

Arabians also have short, straight backs. They have fewer bones in their backs than other horses do. Their tail is set high. It seems to shoot upward from the horse's body. Then it drops like a long, flowing waterfall. The mane is long and flowing, too.

Most Arabians are a solid color—**bay**, **chestnut**, or gray. Some that are very light gray look white. A small number of Arabians are black. Many dark-colored Arabians have white markings on their faces or legs. The purest Arabians have black skin—even if their coats look white! The black skin shows around their eyes.

Arabians are strong, but they are not large. People measure a horse's height at the **withers**. Most Arabians are 56 to 60 inches (142 to 152 centimeters) tall. People also use the word hand to say how tall a horse is. A hand is 4 inches (10 centimeters). Most Arabians are 14 to 15 hands high.

Arabians' eyes are more oval than the eyes of other horses.

This Arabian's coat shines in the sunlight.

Newborn Arabians

Even as babies, Arabians are beautiful. Newborn **foals** have the same shaped heads as the adults. At first, their manes and tails are short and fluffy. Soon they will become long and flowing. A few Arabian foals have a pink **dappled** pattern. This makes them look almost purple! Arabians with this coloring turn white as they get older.

Some Arabians are born dark but get lighter. Gray Arabians start out black, bay, or chestnut. They get lighter as they age—but their skin stays dark.

Arabians are sweet from the beginning. They like to be handled gently. They are not afraid of people. Loud, sudden noises do not scare them easily. Most are them are very willing to please. Children and Arabian foals make friends quickly!

This Arabian foal is running alongside its mother.

Arabians in History

Arabians are a very old **breed**. Horses that looked like Arabians lived in the Middle East long ago. Desert **nomads** had some of the finest of these horses. The nomads were Bedouin (BEH-duh-wun) people. Their horses became the Arabian breed.

Horses that look like Arabians appear in early paintings. Some of these paintings are over 4,000 years old.

The Bedouins' horses were war horses. The Bedouins rode long distances and made quick **raids** on other groups. They needed horses that were fast, strong, and smart. The Bedouins valued their horses and took good care of them. They kept them from mixing with other breeds. And they let only the best ones have babies.

Over time, some Arabian horses ended up in other areas. So did other Middle Eastern horses. They ended up in parts of Europe, Asia, and Africa. Often this happened in times of war. People often captured enemies' horses in battle.

This Arabian is descended from the horses used by Bedouins in the desert.

Europeans saw how good Arabian horses were. They got them whenever they could. Their European horses were heavier and slower. The Arabian horses and European horses had foals together. The Arabians brought speed and **agility** to the heavier European breeds.

By the 1700s, Europeans were bringing Arabian horses from the Middle East. They used them for all sorts of riding, racing, and hunting. And they used Arabians to make other horse breeds better. People started bringing Arabians to North America, too. Through the 1800s and 1900s, Arabians became more and more popular.

Long ago, European knights wore heavy armor. They needed big, heavy war horses. When people stopped wearing armor, they wanted lighter, faster horses.

The first Arabian in the U.S. came to Virginia in 1725. He was the father of more than 300 foals!

You can see this Arabian's thin, triangular face.

What Are Arabians Like?

The Bedouins shared their lives with their horses. This helped the breed in many ways. Life in the desert was hard. The horses grew to be strong. They could live through hot days and cold nights. They could travel a long way without getting tired. They needed little food and water. And they were brave and spirited.

These things are still true today. Arabians are known for being very smart. They are lively riding horses. But they are also easy to handle and train. Their close ties to people have made them loving and gentle. These horses are real people-lovers!

Bedouins' war horses were usually mares. The Bedouin treated their war mares well. Sometimes they brought them into family tents to keep them safe.

Arabians can be very loving and gentle horses.

Arabians at Work

Horseback riding is one of the best-loved sports today. And Arabian owners love to ride their beautiful horses! These horses are good for just about any kind of riding. They are as good for trail riding as they are in horse shows. They are wonderful horses for jumping, parades, and hunting.

Arabians are one of the breeds people call "hot-blooded." Hot-blooded breeds are spirited and fast. Even so, Arabians are easy to work with.

Arabians are good at racing, too. Arabian racing is a growing sport. Arabians also take part in **endurance** races. These races cover long distances. The horses might go 25 to 100 miles (40 to 161 kilometers) in a single day! Sometimes endurance races go on for many days. It takes a strong horse to finish such a race.

Arabians have a big windpipe and good lungs. Getting plenty of air gives them better endurance.

This Arabian has been taught to jump over fences.

Arabians Today

Arabians are one of the world's ten most **popular** breeds. Once, they lived only in the Middle East. But now Arabians live in other parts of the world. People raise them in Europe, Australia, North and South America, and other places.

> In the early 1970s, Arabians became very popular in America. Now most of the world's Arabians live in the U.S.

Arabians are beautiful horses! But they have many other good points, too. They are known for being smart and lively. They are known for their bravery and endurance. They have played an important part in many people's lives.

> Many modern horse breeds are part Arabian. Today's Thoroughbreds can be traced back to three Arabian stallions.

Arabians have been important in the horse world, too. They have added strength, speed, and beauty to many other breeds. The world would not be the same without proud, spirited Arabians.

This lively Arabian is running in a country field.

Body Parts of a Horse

1. Ears
2. Forehead
3. Forelock
4. Eyes
5. Nostril
6. Muzzle
7. Lips
8. Chin
9. Cheek
10. Neck
11. Shoulder
12. Chest
13. Elbow
14. Forearm
15. Chestnut
16. Knee
17. Cannon
18. Pastern
19. Coronet
20. Hoof
21. Barrel
22. Fetlock
23. Hock
24. Tail
25. Gaskin
26. Stifle
27. Point of hip
28. Croup
29. Loin
30. Back
31. Withers
32. Mane
33. Poll

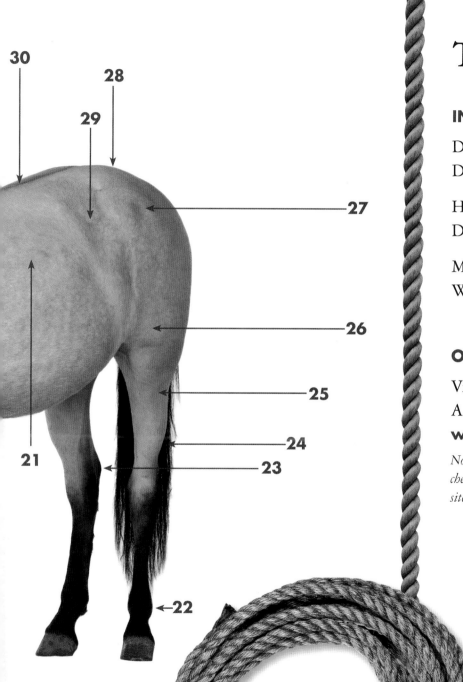

30

28

29

27

26

25

24

23

21

22

To Find Out More

IN THE LIBRARY

Driscoll, Laura. *Horses*. New York: Grosset & Dunlap, 1997.

Hartley Edwards, Elwyn. *Horses*. New York: Dorling Kindersley, 1993.

Micek, Tomas. *Arabian Horses*. Milwaukee, WI: Gareth Stevens, 1995.

ON THE WEB

Visit our Web site for lots of links about Arabians:

www.childsworld.com/links

Note to Parents, Teachers, and Librarians: We routinely check our Web links to make sure they're safe, active sites—so encourage your readers to check them out!

Glossary

agility (uh-JIL-uh-tee) Agility means being able to move quickly and easily. Arabian horses brought agility to some heavier horse breeds.

bay (BAY) A bay horse is brown with a black mane and tail. Many Arabians are bays.

breed (BREED) A breed is a certain type of an animal. Arabians are a well-known horse breed.

chestnut (CHEST-nut) A chestnut horse is reddish brown with a brown mane and tail.

dappled (DAP-puld) Dappled horses have small light and dark patches. Some Arabian foals have pinkish dappling.

endurance (in-DUR-unss) Endurance is being able to keep doing something that is very hard. Arabians are well known for their endurance.

foals (FOHLZ) Foals are baby horses. Arabian foals sometimes change color as they age.

mares (MAYRZ) Mares are female horses. Arabian mares were once used as war horses.

nomads (NOH-madz) Nomads are people who keep moving from place to place. Bedouin nomads raised the first Arabians.

popular (PAH-pyuh-lur) When something is popular, it is liked by lots of people. Arabians are very popular.

raids (RAYDZ) Raids are quick, surprise attacks. Bedouins rode Arabian horses when they went on raids.

withers (WIH-thurz) The withers is the high spot above a horse's shoulders. An Arabian's height is measured at the withers.

Index

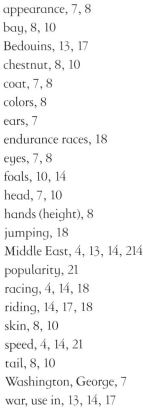